CORNISH COLLECTION

Published by Truran, Croft Prince, Mount Hawke, Truro, Cornwall. TR48EE
www.truranbooks.co.uk

Printed by R. Booth Ltd, Antron Hill, Mabe, Penryn, Cornwall. TR109HH

ISBN 1 85022 165 0 (cased)
ISBN 1 85022 166 9 (paperback)

The publishers gratefully acknowledge the co-operation of The National Trust in Cornwall in the preparation of this book.

For information about the work of the National Trust in Cornwall; and for details of the opening times of properties please ring 0120874281

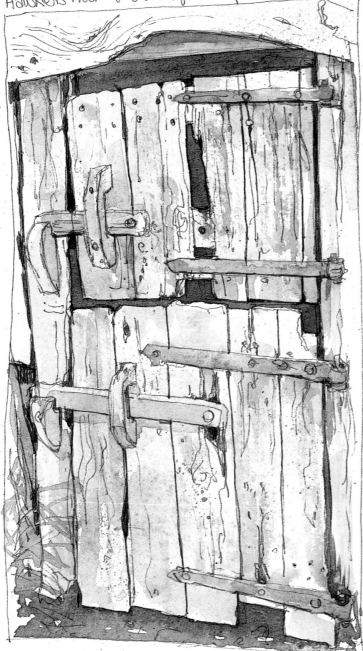

Hawker's hut at Vicarage cliff, Morwenstow
This is about as far away from home as I can go in Cornwall — so its either
the end or the beginning . . . The Rev. Hawker used to sit here & smoke
opium & write poems & look out for wrecks. The cliffs & the reefs
here are terrifying. On my right — beyond a small bank of blackthorn,
the cliff drops away for hundreds of feet . . .

4

cotehele.

This strange tower stands on a hill behind
cotehele House. I almost reached it - but got
soaked in a sudden squall r retreated.

5

the Mount cat!

the Causeway

6

I had to wait for the tide to drop to walk across the causeway to the Mount. Strong S.W. wind — the only shelter behind the huge quay walls.

NATIONAL
MARITIME
MUSEUM
at
COTEHELE QUAY
in association with
THE NATIONAL TRUST

8

Its so hard to pick just a few images from a January day at Cotehele Quay. Brilliant light on the river, soft silky mud as the tide drops. The last Tamar sailing barge pulled up near a tiny fishing boat. The strings in the quay the ferns in the wall... And I didn't even walk to the wall...

ODDITIES ~ frightening gargoyles
& friendly-looking lions at Trerice

A 'squint' by what was once the main entrance into cotehele.

A lead water tank in the kitchen court at Cotehele.

The coat of arms above the door at Lanhydrock

I turned to take a last look at Cotehele & noticed this sundial.

6 5
7 4
8 3
9 · 10 · 11 · 12 · 1 · 2

this is outside the kitchen quarters at Lanhydrock

130
120
110 FEVER HEAT
100 BLOOD HEAT
90
80 SUMMER HEAT
70
60
50 TEMPE RATE
40
30 FREEZ ING
20
10
0 ZERO

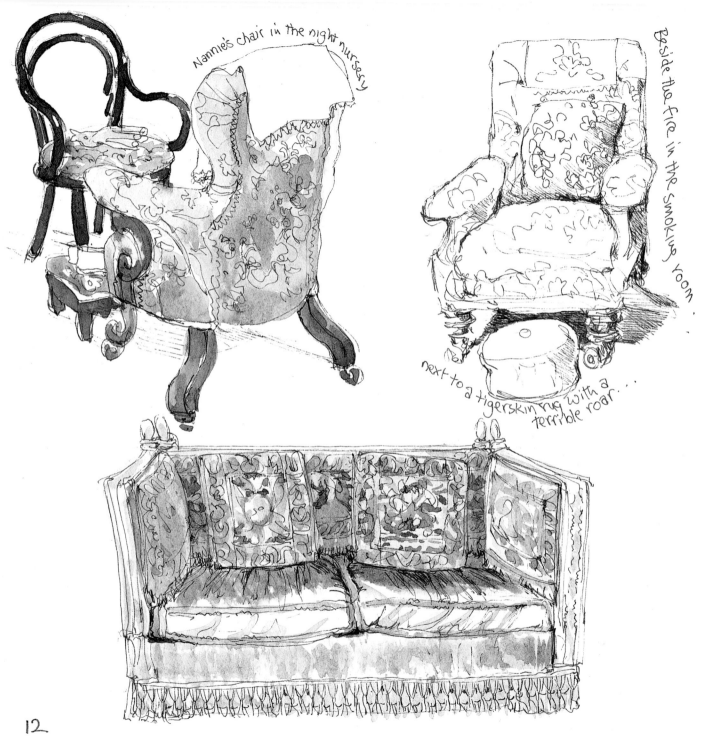

Nannie's chair in the night nursery

Beside the fire in the smoking room .

next to a tigerskin rug with a terrible roar...

12

Her Ladyship's chair

some very elegant sofas in the drawing room at Lanhydrock

13

14

Cotswold has masses of different styles & ages of windows. The house has grown & changed so much over the years

15

lots of wonderful doors at Cotehele

16

and slightly grander ones at Lanhydrock

17

Cotehele

Trerice

All the big houses have their own
atmosphere. I feel at home in both
Trerice & Cotehele. Cotehele especially —
with its dark rooms & panelling & lovely
tapestries. Lanhydrock is big & grand &
brings to mind the last years before the
first war. I love the kitchens there —
I must have been either a servant or
an Elizabethan in a past life!

19

The Old Post Office. Tintagel — marooned amongst modest housing & shops

A couple of oddities —
this one, up a tiny alley
in Port Isaac — for slim, agile
people only I should think.

And the tower at Trelissick —
it just has to come out of a
fairytale, with Rapunzel's
window at the very top...

21

The best way to approach Lanhydrock is along the straight avenue from
Respryn & the gatehouse is the first thing you see. It's part of the
original house - before the fire - & my favourite part. On the first
floor is a beautiful room of pale wood & stone & a feeling of peace.
All the pointy turrets & balls (an architectural term !?) & the topiary
beyond remind me always of Alice in Wonderland. I haven't read
it for years, but I can visualise the Red Queen here...

The view down the creek on a perfectly still January day

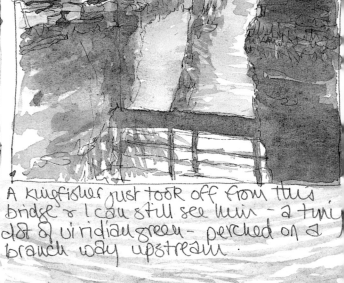

A kingfisher just took off from this bridge & I can still see him - a tiny dot of viridian green - perched on a branch way upstream.

This is a peaceful spot now with nothing disturbing the water but the ducks! Its hard to imagine what it must have been like with boats tied up alongside the quays, people busy unloading & the lime kilns working.

PONT
Nr. Polruan

NOTICE
____

Dues for discharging or
shipping over these quays
will be collected as follows,

Grain 1ᵈ per Quarter
Timber 3ᵈ per Load.
Manures 3ᵈ per Ton
Sand 2ᵈ Coal 3ᵈ

Other goods in like pro-
portion.

Wᴹ PEASE
Steward.

Dated Lostwithiel May 19th 1894.

I can't resist this sign
It's so hard to imagine these
quays busy with boats &
people

25

For **HOUSEMAID** ring once

STILLROOM and

DAIRYMAID " twice

KITCHENMAID three times

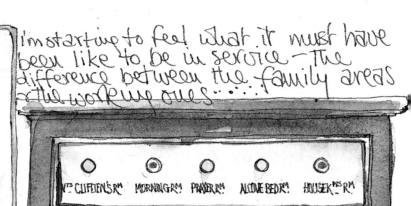

I'm starting to feel what it must have been like to be in service — the difference between the family areas & the working ones......

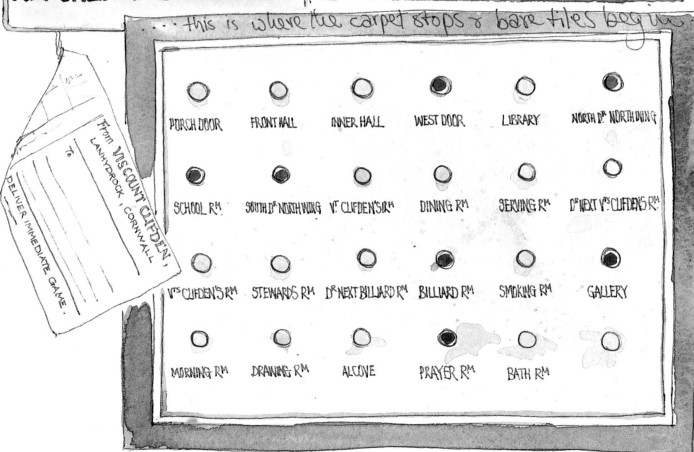

...this is where the carpet stops & bare tiles begin

Please SHUT THIS DOOR QUIETLY

KENT'S Knife Cleaner with IMPROVEMENTS Patented 1865 AND 1870

water coolers, lemon squeezers, tin openers...

kitchens with all mod-cons knife cleaners tongue presses

S. NYE & Co. MANUFACTURERS LONDON

HOT WATER

JEAKES' Gt RUSSELL St BLOOMSBURY

A lion & a unicorn on every door

...and, of course, cooks, scullery maids & dairy maids

KENT PATENTEE & MANUFACTURERS 199 HIGH HOLBORN LONDON

D.C.L. YEAST SOLE MANUFACTURERS The Distillers Co Ltd EDINBURGH

FOLLOWS BATE LTD "CROWN" No 2 TONGUE & MEAT PRESS MAKERS MANCHESTER

27

Durgan.
A quiet walk
through trees
to a hidden
spot on the
Helford.

28

The old School House sits directly above the beach.
How did they ever work with that view outside?
Having just replaced a 'scantle' roof
at home - I'm fascinated by the
decorative slates on the roof &
the gable ends.

Almost all of these clocks are at Lanhydrock

Trerice

It must have been an important job — keeping all these wound

I think this is the oldest clock still in its
original position (& still telling the time)

Treue

nursery clock

And keeping them to time   Perhaps most people did not have
personal watches then & so needed so many clocks in every room

31

The stables at Trelissick - lots of warm bricks & flat-topped arched doorways

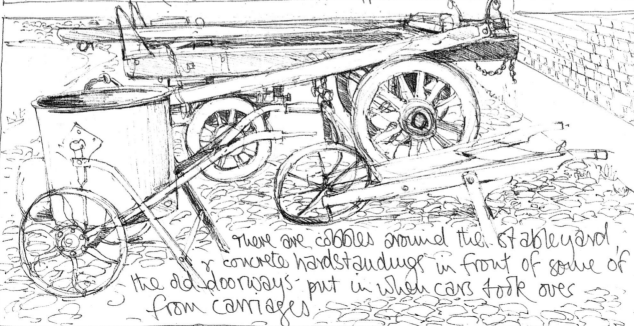

There are cobbles around the stableyard, & concrete hardstandings in front of some of the old doorways - put in when cars took over from carriages

33

These two stand either side of a large fireplace & have never been this close before.

Both Lanhydrock & Trerice have lots of this wonderful work..

34

i'm getting dizzy looking up at the plasterwork ceilings...

These lovely ladies are part of one of the tapestries at Cotehele. I've never seen a house so full of tapestries, which somehow make the rooms dark, but cosy with an ancient, almost sombre feel... (which I love...)

35

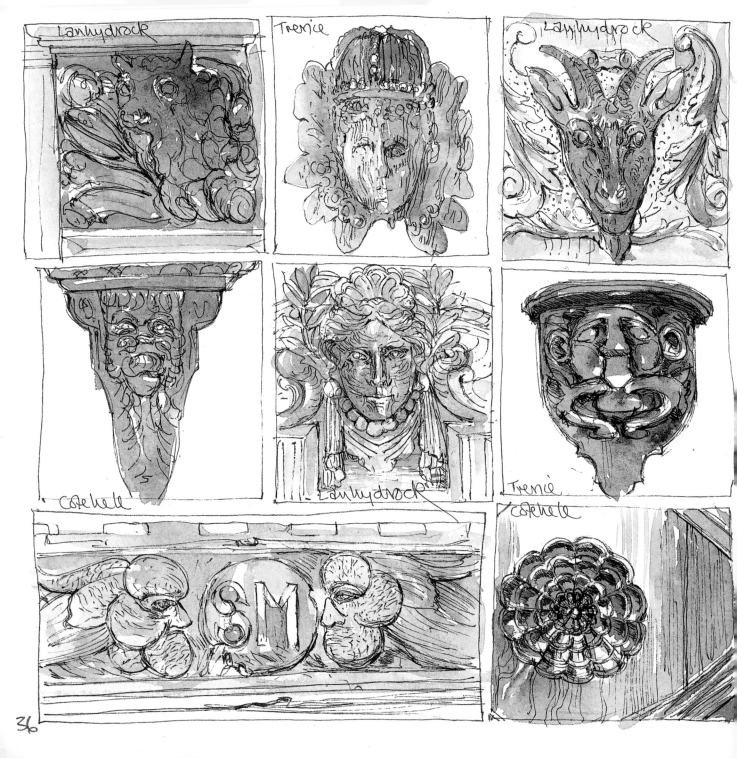

Lanhydrock

Trerice

Lanhydrock

Cotehele

Lanhydrock

Trerice
Cotehele

SM

These are just a tiny selection of all the carved panels, furniture & decorations.

Adam & Eve & a very stern guard who obviously didn't do his job very well.... at Carlisle.

A saint (I think) who kept a dragon as a pet. And strange observers in the castle.

37

Jugs everywhere. Plain white in the dairy, blue & white on the dresser, enamel & glass & pewter.

No plastic or horrible cardboard cartons.

I've used a little churn just like this one....

38

I especially like the little verdigried bell pushes at Lamb's duck

39

Trevice

40

cotehele

Glass must have been a revelation in these houses..
r such a status symbol. The huge window at Trerice would
have been a wonder. Each piece of old glass is so much more
beautiful than the flawless, plain glass we have today

41

KEEPING CLEAN ~ shiny marble r glass, beautiful jugs, expensive soap, eau de cologne

Lead r brass, scrubbing brushes, enamel soap dishes, Golden Ingot soap, Snowene cleaner

Bay Rhum, Lavender water,
Eau de Cologne
English violet,
Eau de Portugal,
Rose & boric eye lotion

camphorated oil,
Eno Fruit salt
Ellimans Universal
embrocation
Evans throat
pastilles

43

Trerice
on a warm autumn morning. the lanes round here are tiny & once you arrive
its like stepping back in time. No traffic noise, just me & the birds..
imagination working overtime! I would like to live here....
44

Beautiful stonework at Trerice.

The fishermen's huts don't look as if they were built—
they just grew here, in corners, on odd bits of
land, made of driftwood & rocks from
the cliffs

Priest's Cove, Cape Cornwall

46

carpet of 'hottentot fig' has sprawled down the cliff, to cover the roof of this hut.

47

St. Michael's Mount must be one of the most pictured (& romantic) places in Cornwall. This page was completed when, yesterday, I saw it lit up by the setting sun & looking like a fairytale stage set. When I got to Marazion the sun had gone, but as compensation I got to see a glorious yellow & gold sunset & the starlings dancing & swirling over the marshes on the way to their roosts.

48

A suitable ending I think...